Michel de Verteuil CSSp

Meditating on the Mysteries

The Rosary as Biblical Prayer

DEV

VERITAS

First published in 1996 by
Archdiocesan Pastoral Centre
2 Carmody Road
St Augustine
Trinidad
West Indies

This edition published in 1997 by
Veritas Publications
7-8 Lower Abbey Street
Dublin 1

na # 5991
(6068)

ISBN 1 85390 392 2

British Library Cataloguing
in Publication Data.
A catalogue record for
this book is available
from the British Library.

Cover design by Lucia Happel
Printed in the Republic of Ireland by Betaprint Ltd, Dublin

Contents

As for Mary, she treasured all these things and pondered them in her heart.

Luke 2:19

Donation

Foreword

The Rosary has been the favourite prayer of Catholics for centuries. It has been the object of many encyclical letters and apostolic exhortations from various popes.

It is found in the hands of tried and trusted old people who find strength and consolation as the beads slip through their fingers.

It is taught to little children as soon as they have learnt the Our Father, Hail Mary and Glory be.

Anything, therefore, that will help people to understand a little more deeply what the Rosary is all about, it most welcome.

Michel de Verteuil has once more provided us with thought-provoking material, this time in the form of meditations on the mysteries of the Rosary, this most beloved prayer.

May this little booklet be abundantly blessed in its desired effect, that is, to help us to meditate on the mysteries, imitate what they contain and obtain what they promise.

Queen of the Holy Rosary, pray for us.

✠ Anthony Pantin
Archbishop of Port of Spain

The Method of Lectio Divina

The prayers proposed here are the fruit of *Lectio divina,* a method of meditative bible reading which goes back to the early centuries of our Church, and continues to be a source of deep spiritual growth.

Lectio divina (a Latin expression which means *sacred reading*) is done in **three** stages:

Reading: You read the passage slowly and reverently, allowing the words to sink into your consciousness. If necessary you clarify the meaning of words or expressions that you are not familiar with.

Meditation: You allow the passage to stir up memories within you so that you recognise in it your own experience or that of people who have touched your life.

Prayer: You allow the meditation to lead you to prayer: thanksgiving, humility and petition.

The prayers given here are models. You can use them as they are but they will also suggest ways in which you can pray from your own meditations; you will then be practising *Lectio divina.*

Now and then the prayers are preceded by quotations from well-known thinkers or spiritual writers. The quotations are there to remind us that through Bible reading we enter into the wisdom of humanity.

We practice *Lectio divina* most fruitfully when we do it in conjunction with the Church's Sunday lectionary, spending the week with the gospel passage for the following Sunday. By doing this our personal prayer life becomes integrated into the prayer of the Church, and reaches its high point each Sunday in the parish liturgy.

Introduction

The Second Vatican Council laid down that devotion to the Blessed Virgin Mary should be guided by 'Sacred Scripture, the Holy Fathers, the doctors and the liturgy of the Church' (*Lumen gentium*, 67).

This booklet attempts to apply this guideline of the Council to the recitation of the Rosary, that most popular of all devotions to the Blessed Virgin. Its purpose is to help people integrate the Rosary with their love for Sacred Scripture.

In the prayer, which by tradition we say at the conclusion of the Rosary, we ask that

> *meditating on these mysteries,*
> *we may imitate what they contain,*
> *and obtain what they promise.*

This is a very ancient liturgical prayer, totally in accord with the teaching of the Council, and reflecting a deep understanding of how to say the Rosary.

According to this prayer, the fifteen 'mysteries' are sacred stories; through 'meditation' we enter into these stories and let them carry us forward into a deeper, richer life, already here on earth, but leading us to the 'promise' of their fulfilment in heaven.

The prayer is clearly based on the traditional form of bible reading called *Lectio divina* which is outlined on page 6.

The meditations proposed here link each mystery to a Bible passage. At times the passage is rather long and I have, therefore, been selective, and focused whenever possible on the role of the Blessed Virgin in the story.

In each case, the passages chosen are only one possibility. I hope that readers will be led to look at other passages too, thus enriching further their recitation of the Rosary.

The Joyful Mysteries

This first in the three groups of mysteries invites us to meditate on the birth and infancy of Jesus, as related in the first chapters of St Luke's Gospel.

It is important to interpret these infancy narratives correctly, as meditations on the whole life of Jesus, not merely one part of it. The events we read about there were a fulfilment of Old Testament stories and would recur many times in the adult life of Jesus and the New Testament Church.

These are truly 'mysteries', therefore, events that are being fulfilled today 'even as we listen'. We read in them the 'joyful' manifestations of God's presence in our world, pointing the way forward for us and the whole of humanity.

First Joyful Mystery

The Annunciation

GOSPEL TEXT

Luke 1:26-38
The Annunciation
In the sixth month the angel Gabriel was sent by God to a town in Galilee called Nazareth, to a virgin betrothed to a man named Joseph, of the House of David; and the virgin's name was Mary. He went in and said to her, 'Rejoice, you who enjoy God's favour! The Lord is with you.' She was deeply disturbed by these words and asked herself what this greeting could mean, but the angel said to her, 'Mary, do not be afraid; you have won God's favour. Look! You are to conceive in your womb and bear a son, and you must name him Jesus. He will be great and will be called Son of the Most High. The Lord God will give him the throne of his ancestor David; he will rule over the House of Jacob for ever and his reign will have no end.' Mary said to the angel, 'But how can this come about, since I have no knowledge of man?' The angel answered, 'the Holy Spirit will come upon you, and the power of the Most High will cover you with its shadow. And so the child will be holy and will be called the Son of God. And I tell you this too: your cousin Elizabeth also, in her old age, has conceived a son, and she whom people called barren is now in her sixth month, *for nothing is impossible to God.*' Mary said, 'you see before you the Lord's servant, let it happen to me as you have said'. And the angel left her.

MEDITATION

The Annunciation is the story of the Blessed Virgin Mary's spiritual journey, starting with the angel's greeting and culminating in her humble acceptance of God's will for her and the angel's departure.

It is the journey travelled by all those who receive a call from God as attested to by many similar stories told in the Bible.

We too make the journey whenever God calls us to a new stage in our life journey, in our relationship with him or with those close to us, in a task we undertake, a new commitment.

The gospel account is over very quickly but the corresponding journey in real life could last months or even years.

We can distinguish five stages in the journey:

verses 26-30	the first encounter, giving rise as always in the Bible to a combination of awe and reassurance;
verses 31-33	the angel announces a mission in the context of the fulfilment of God's promises;
verses 34-37	a dialogue conducted with the utmost reverence on either side;
verse 38	the final acceptance, humble and serene, of God's will.

PRAYERS

Lord, we thank you for the time when you led us on a journey by which we eventually accepted to make a radical change in our lives:

- *we decided to get married or enter the religious life;*
- *we came to terms with illness;*
- *we gave up a friendship that was doing us harm;*
- *we accepted a subordinate position in our parish or workplace;*
- *we were able to forgive.*

We remember the day when we realised that you were calling us to something new.

Like Mary we were deeply disturbed at this word and asked ourselves what it could mean.

Many times we asked the question, how could this come about? Gradually we understood that it was really the work of your Spirit, that something great and wonderful would be born, which had been in preparation for a long time.

*We thought of how you had done similar things for people we had
known and that nothing is impossible to you.*
*Then one day we realised that we were nothing but your humble
servants and we let your word carry out its purpose in us.*
Thank you, Lord.

'Political and technical solutions are useful but will lead to
nothing if they are not reinforced by a radical intellectual
renewal and a moral unification.'
Mikhail Gorbachev
Meeting of World Religious Leaders, September 1993

*Lord, as we look around the world today we see evil triumphing on
every side.*
*We pray that your Church may be your angel sent by you to remind
a disturbed humanity that your Son Jesus is greater than every evil,
that he must sit on the throne of his ancestor David and his reign
will have no end,*
*that your Spirit continues to cover the earth with its shadow, so
that your holy work may be born.*
*We are merely your humble servants allowing what you have said to
be done to us.*

*Lord, we pray for pregnant women, especially those who resent
having conceived.*
*Remind them that the child in their womb is holy, will be called a
child of God, is destined to sit on the throne of David their ancestor
and will have a reign that is without end.*

*Lord, from time to time in the midst of our daily occupations you
send us an angel as you did for Mary,*
telling us that we are deeply blessed,
that we have a lofty destiny
and will bring forth what is holy into the world

and we feel confident that the word spoken to us will be fulfilled.
Then the angel leaves us and we go our way alone.

'In the last analysis, history is the record of how individuals
respond to the challenge of their times.'

Sir Arthur Lewis

Lord, we thank you for great people who, like Mary,
see themselves as humble servants,
receiving the challenges of life as a word from you,
which through them will bear fruit in the world.

Second Joyful Mystery

The Visitation

Luke 1:39-46

Mary set out that time and went as quickly as she could into the hill country to a town in Judah. She went into Zechariah's house and greeted Elizabeth. Now it happened that as soon as Elizabeth heard Mary's greeting, the child leapt in her womb and Elizabeth was filled with the Holy Spirit. She gave a loud cry and said, 'Of all women you are the most blessed, and blessed is the fruit of your womb. Why should I be honoured with a visit from the mother of my Lord? Look, the moment your greeting reached my ears, the child in my womb leapt for joy. Yes, blessed is she who believed that the promise made her by the Lord would be fulfilled.'

And Mary said: 'My soul proclaims the greatness of the Lord and my spirit rejoices in God my Saviour.'

MEDITATION

The gospel story of the Visitation is highly symbolic. It is the encounter of two women of faith, each bringing out the best in each other.

Mary in her pregnancy is the symbol of God's people, bearing his presence within them as the Bible continually reminds us, and conveying blessings to the world as it had been prophesied of Abraham, our ancestor in the faith *(Genesis 12:3)*.

The passage stresses the power of Mary's greeting *(verses 40, 41 and 44)*; there is no mention of the words she spoke, her attitude was all.

PRAYERS

Lord, there are times when we feel discouraged.

We know we have possibilities within us or at our disposal from others, but somehow or other we don't feel capable of achieving anything.

Then you send people like Mary to us, people of hope who believe that whatever promise you make to us will be fulfilled,

and from the moment their greeting reaches our ears,

all that is within us leaps for joy and we know we are filled with your Holy Spirit.

Lord, as we meditate on this mystery, the women of our nation come before our eyes.

We see homes where neighbours are visiting each other,

all of them people of faith, with the potential to bring forth a new kind of society.

Their mutual greetings are joyful as they welcome each other with blessings,

they give each other the courage to believe that the promises you make are always fulfilled.

Lord, many times it has happened that we went to visit someone, thinking that we were going to bless them:

- *a sick person in hospital;*
- *a family which had suffered bereavement;*
- *a community which we considered abandoned;*

but they greeted us with reverence and humility,

as Elizabeth greeted Mary, and we felt so blessed that we glorified you for having looked on our lowliness.

Lord, we thank you for Mary. Truly, of all women she is the most blessed and blessed is the fruit of her womb.

'If Christians cultivate openness and allow themselves to be tested, they will gather the fruits of dialogue, and will discover with admiration all that God's action through Jesus Christ in his spirit has accomplished and continues to accomplish in the world.'

Vatican Document, Dialogue and Proclamation

Lord, many people, especially those of other faiths, are afraid of our Church.
they think that we are always out to convert them or to prove that we are superior to them; we make them feel less than they are capable of.
Teach us to come to others as Mary did,
so that merely by our greeting the potential that is within them will leap for joy, they will be aware that they are filled with your Holy Spirit and we ourselves will be blessed.

Third Joyful Mystery

The Nativity

GOSPEL TEXT

Luke 2:1-20

The Birth of Jesus and the visit of the shepherds

Now it happened that at this time Caesar Augustus issued a decree that a census should be made of the whole inhabited world. This census – the first – took place while Quirinius was governor of Syria, and everyone went to be registered, each to his own town. So Joseph set out from the town of Nazareth in Galilee for Judaea, to David's town called Bethlehem, since he was of David's House and line, in order to be registered together with Mary, his betrothed, who was with child. Now it happened that, while they were there, the time came for her to have her child, and she gave birth to a son, her first-born. She wrapped him in swaddling clothes and laid him in a manger because there was no room for them in the living-space. In the countryside close by there were shepherds out in the fields keeping guard over their sheep during the watches of the night. An angel of the Lord stood over them and the glory of the Lord shone round them. They were terrified, but the angel said, 'Do not be afraid. Look, I bring you news of great joy, a joy to be shared by the whole people. Today in the town of David a Saviour has been born to you; he is Christ the Lord. And here is a sign for you: you will find a baby wrapped in swaddling clothes and lying in a manger.' And all at once with the angel there was a great throng of the hosts of heaven, praising God with the words:

> Glory to God in the highest heaven,
> and on earth peace for those he favours.

Now it happened that when the angels had gone from them into heaven, the shepherds said to one another, 'Let us go to Bethlehem and see this event which the Lord has made known to us.' So they hurried away and found Mary and Joseph, and the baby lying in the manger. When they saw the child they repeated what they had been told about him, and everyone who heard it was astonished at what the shepherds said to them. As for Mary, she treasured all these things and pondered them in her heart. And the shepherds went back glorifying and praising God for all they had heard and seen, just as they had been told.

MEDITATION

This well-known story is very rich so we will focus on some aspects only. In these meditations we are staying with the perspective of the Blessed Virgin, especially in *verses 6-7,* and *verses 16-20.*

In *verses 6-7* St Luke insists that Mary gave birth 'when the time came for her to have her child'. Contrary to the popular interpretation he indicates no regret that there was no room in the inn. All happened as was foretold.

To understand the significance of *verse 19,* it is important to note that the Greek work which we translate 'things' is *rhema,* which means both 'word' and 'event'. Mary, through her interior attitude of respectful listening, turns the event into a sacred word.

PRAYERS

'Nothing happens before its time.'

Trinidad folk saying

Lord, we pray for those who are involved in lofty projects and are becoming impatient
- *parish youth leaders are not getting co-operation;*
- *a new party won no seats in the election;*
- *parents are trying in vain to dialogue with their teenagers.*
Help us to remember Mary, how when the time came for her to have her child she gave birth to a son.

*She was at peace, felt no great concern that there was no room for
them in the inn,*
*merely wrapped him in swaddling clothes and laid him in a
manger.*

Lord, these days we are all very busy.
*At work or in school we have to expend much effort to achieve
success.*
*At home we are bombarded with information from television and
radio.*
*We have time only for the sensational and allow the ordinary events
of life to come and go:*
- *the signs of maturity in our children;*
- *the life crises of those close to us;*
- *new stirrings of resentment or of hope among the ordinary
people of the country.*

*Even in our relationship with you we concentrate on the miraculous
and the extraordinary,*
*glorify and praise you because things turn out exactly as we were
told they would.*
Mary teaches us on the contrary to see in every event a call to grow,
a sacred word you have spoken to us,
to be welcomed as a treasure and pondered within our hearts,
reflected on and integrated into our consciousness.
Lord, help us to be more like Mary.

**'My cell will not be one of stone nor wood but of self-
knowledge.'**

St Catherine of Siena

*Lord, we thank you for all the contemplatives in the world, both
those in enclosed convents and those called, like Mary, to live
within their families and in secular surroundings.*
While others chatter and repeat endlessly what they have been told,

they, like Mary, know how to be silent, treasuring things and pondering them in their hearts.

Fourth Joyful Mystery

The Presentation of Jesus in the Temple

GOSPEL TEXT

Luke 2:22-40

Jesus is presented in the Temple

And when the day came for them to be purified in keeping with the Law of Moses, they took him up to Jerusalem to present him to the Lord – observing what is written in the Law of the Lord: *Every first-born male must be consecrated to the Lord* – and also to offer in sacrifice, in accordance with what is prescribed in the Law of the Lord, *a pair of turtledoves or two young pigeons.* Now in Jerusalem there was a man named Simeon. He was an upright and devout man; he looked forward to the restoration of Israel and the Holy Spirit rested on him. It had been revealed to him by the Holy Spirit that he would not see death until he had set eyes on the Christ of the Lord. Prompted by the Spirit he came to the Temple; and when the parents brought in the child Jesus to do for him what the Law required, he took him into his arms and blessed God; and he said:

The Nunc Dimittis

> Now, Master, you are letting your servant go in peace as you promised;
> for my eyes have seen the salvation
> which you have made ready in the sight of the nations;
> a light of revelation for the gentiles
> and glory for your people Israel.

The prophecy of Simeon

As the child's father and mother were wondering at the things that were being said about him, Simeon blessed them and said to Mary his mother, 'Look, he is destined for the fall and rise of many in Israel, destined to be a sign that is opposed – and a sword will pierce your soul too – so that the secret thoughts of many may be laid bare.'

The prophecy of Anna

There was a prophetess, too, Anna the daughter of Phanuel, of the tribe of Asher. She was well on in years. Her days of girlhood over, she had been married for seven years before becoming a widow. She was now eighty-four years old and never left the Temple, serving God night and day with fasting and prayer. She came up just at that moment and began to praise God; and she spoke of the child to all who looked forward to the deliverance of Jerusalem.

The hidden life of Jesus at Nazareth

When they had done everything the Law of the Lord required, they went back to Galilee, to their own town of Nazareth. And as the child grew to maturity, he was filled with wisdom; and God's favour was with him.

MEDITATION

As in the previous mystery the gospel text is long and we must stay with some aspects only.

It is highly significant that when Jesus enters the Temple the priests are absent. Simeon and Anna are symbols of God's faithful ones, having no official status and yet (or perhaps therefore) free enough to recognise the decisive moment of grace for their people and all humanity.

It is also significant that the Holy Family are among the poor who are excused from the more expensive sacrifices and are allowed to bring 'a pair of turtle doves or two young pigeons' (Leviticus 5:7; 12:8).

As throughout his first two chapters St Luke stresses here that everything is done 'according to the Law of the Lord'.

PRAYERS

Lord, we go through life just living day to day as best we can
- *bringing up children;*
- *doing our jobs;*
- *socialising with friends, going to parties, playing games;*
- *going to Church and doing our bit in the parish.*

Then, every once in a while you send us someone,
a distant relative, a friend, a spiritual guide,
who does for us what Simeon did for Mary and Joseph,
welcomes us with enthusiasm,
blesses us for fulfilling a long-held hope for the world,
leaving us surprised and wondering at these wonderful things said
about us.

'Do not suppose that I have come to bring peace to the earth;
it is not peace I have come to bring but a sword.'

Matthew 1-:34

Lord, forgive us for making the message of Jesus so comfortable,
a word that tells us we don't have to try and change the world we
live in because it will never be different.
We pray that your Church will be like Simeon proclaiming to all
that Jesus comes into the world to separate good from evil,
to exalt virtues like humility, generosity and trust which are not
valued,
and to confront arrogance, meanness and self-centredness wherever
they are found.
As for us who, like Mary, are called to bring Jesus into the world,
a sword of sorrow will pierce our hearts, because through our words
the deep-seated prejudices of many will be laid bare.

'The secular school explains things and creates knowledge, the
religious school teaches how to contemplate things and creates
wonder.'

Anthony de Mello

Lord, often those who follow our education programmes, both in school and parishes, are not taught to see the world with new eyes; like everyone else they are dazzled by power and wealth and set great store by them.

We pray that these programmes will be temples out of which people like Simeon will emerge,

able to recognise that a small group of humble people coming to do what the Law requires,

are the men and women who are the hope for the future, the light of the world and the glory of your people Israel.

Fifth Joyful Mystery

The Finding of Jesus in the Temple

GOSPEL TEXT

Luke 2:41-52

Jesus among the doctors of the Law

Every year his parents used to go to Jerusalem for the feast of the Passover. When he was twelve years old, they went up for the feast as usual. When the days of the feast were over and they set off for home, the boy Jesus stayed behind in Jerusalem without his parents knowing it. They assumed he was somewhere in the party, and it was only after a day's journey that they went to look for him among their relations and acquaintances. When they failed to find him they went back to Jerusalem looking for him everywhere.

It happened that, three days later, they found him in the Temple, sitting among the teachers, listening to them, and asking them questions; and all those who heard him were astounded at his intelligence and his replies. They were overcome when they saw him, and his mother said to him, 'My child, why have you done this to us? See how worried your father and I have been, looking for you.' He replied, 'Why were you looking for me? Did you not know that I must be in my Father's house?' But they did not understand what he meant.

The hidden life of Nazareth resumed

He went down with them and came to Nazareth and lived under their authority. His mother stored up all these things in her heart. And Jesus increased in wisdom, in stature, and in favour with God and with people.

MEDITATION

Another highly symbolical story. We can read it from the point of view of either Jesus or his parents.

The two sections of the story, *verses 41-50,* on the one hand, and *51-52,* on the other, can be meditated on separately.

Taken together, however, and understood as complementing each other, they give a balanced picture of the role of authority in human life.

PRAYERS

*Lord, we pray today for all those involved in the work of education
– parents, teachers, youth leaders, church ministers.
Young people come to stay with us and live under our authority for
a time, increasing in wisdom, in stature, and in favour with you
and with men and women.
But they are not ours, you are their father and they must be busy
about your affairs.
some of them have unusual vocations,
in the Church perhaps, or in art or politics.
At times we will feel we have lost them and be overcome
with worry as we spend days looking for them.
Then quite unexpectedly we find them at ease in their temple,
asking and answering questions, quite surprised
that we should be looking for them, while we remain
perplexed at what it all means.
Lord, bringing up children is a lofty calling; help us, like Mary and
Joseph, to be faithful to it.*

'It may be that the salvation of the world lies with the
maladjusted.'

Martin Luther King

*Lord, there are times in life when we must step out on our own,
knowing that dear ones will be very worried looking for us and
wanting to bring us back to Nazareth where we can be subject to them.
Give us the grace to commit ourselves like Jesus to what we know to
be our Father's business.*

'The Church must be concerned not just with herself, and her relationship of union with God, but with human beings as they really are today.'

Pope Paul VI
concluding the Second Vatican Council, December 1965

Lord, as a Church we tend to remain within our own concerns,
safe in Nazareth where we know the rules of the game, who is
subject to whom,
and we can feel sure we are growing in wisdom, in stature and in
favour with God and with the influential people in society.
We pray that your Church may take the risk of being lost for days
at a time, even though its leaders are overcome with worry,
so that Jesus can be among the learned people of our time,
listening to them and asking them questions,
and modern generations like previous ones can be astounded by the
wisdom of his message and the replies he brings to the problems of
our time.

'Only one ship is seeking us, a black-
sailed unfamiliar, towing at her back
a huge and birdless silence. In her wake
no waters breed or break.'

West Indian Poem, 'Next, Please'

Lord, when we are young we have lofty goals for ourselves.
We are in Jerusalem, at the centre of things, questioning the wisdom
of our day and astounding all by the intelligence of our replies.
Then another time comes when we find ourselves stagnant,
not going anywhere or achieving anything, subject to the
conventions and prejudices of society.
Teach us, Lord, that this too is a necessary stage where, like Jesus in
Nazareth, we can increase in wisdom, in stature and in favour
with you.

The Sorrowful Mysteries

For the gospels, the passion of Jesus is not one moment among many in his life. It is the 'paschal mystery', his journey through death to new life which is the key to his whole life and all his teachings.

Furthermore, each individual 'mystery' of the passion contains in itself the whole 'paschal mystery'.

By meditating on the sorrowful mysteries we enter into the life and teaching of Jesus.

In the gospel narratives, details are often given to show that Jesus was the fulfilment of Old Testament texts, and going back to them will give depth to our meditations.

I suggest remaining with one gospel account and I have chosen Matthew's. We need not be afraid of losing out by limiting ourselves in this way; by going deeply into one gospel we discover all the others.

First Sorrowful Mystery
The Agony in the Garden

GOSPEL TEXT

Matthew 26:36-46
Gethsemane

Then Jesus came with them to a plot of land called Gethsemane; and he said to his disciples, 'Stay here while I go over there to pray.' He took Peter and the two sons of Zebedee with him. And he began to feel sadness and anguish.

Then he said to them, 'My soul is sorrowful to the point of death. Wait here and stay awake with me.' And going on a little further he fell on his face and prayed. 'My father', he said, 'if it is possible, let this cup pass me by. Nevertheless, let it be as you, not I, would have it.' He came back to the disciples and found them sleeping, and he said to Peter, 'So you had not the strength to stay awake with me for one hour? Stay awake, and pray not to be put to the test. The spirit is willing enough, but human nature is weak.' Again, a second time, he went away and prayed: 'My Father', he said, 'if this cup cannot pass by, but I must drink it, your will be done!' And he came back again and found them sleeping, their eyes were so heavy. Leaving them there, he went away again and prayed for the third time, repeating the same words. Then he came back to the disciples and said to them, 'You can sleep on now and have your rest. Look, the hour has come when the Son of man is to be betrayed into the hands of sinners. Get up! Let us go! Look, my betrayer is not far away.'

MEDITATION

The agony in the garden is the story of Jesus' journey from anguish and fear to the point where he accepts the will of the Father and calmly faces his betrayer. A helpful parallel is found in *John 12:27-30.*

In a secondary way, it is the story of the apostles who prove unable to follow Jesus on his journey. It is clearly St Matthew's intention to show that Jesus himself prayed the prayer he taught his disciples and which we now call rightly the 'Lord's Prayer', e.g. 'pray that you not be put to the test' in *verse 41,* and 'your will be done' in *verse 42.*

In the famous saying in *verse 41,* the 'spirit' is the deepest and noblest part of ourselves, and 'the flesh' refers to all our sinful tendencies. *Romans 7:5-25* is a good commentary on the saying.

PRAYERS

Lord, take away our false pride.
Teach us to accept like Jesus that times come when such sadness
comes over us and such great distress that our souls are sorrowful to
the point of death,
and we need close friends to wait and keep watch with us.

'Walk the dark ways of faith and you will attain the vision of God.'

St Augustine

Lord, we remember with gratitude times of crisis when we just fell
on our faces and prayed that if it were possible you would let the
cup pass us by.
Then, somehow or other, we found the resources to add, let it be as
you, not we, would have it.

Lord, you want us to accompany Jesus in the garden by making our
own spiritual journey to accepting your will.
This means having the courage to face up to our own poverty:
* *our lack of trust in you*
* *the people in our lives whom we haven't forgiven*
* *our failures at work or at home.*

We will feel sadness and distress so great that our souls will be sorrowful to the point of death.
But if we persevere, we eventually find that, like Jesus, we can get up and go to face whatever betrayals life has in store for us, letting others sleep and take their rest.

Lord, we expend a lot of energy on our own problems:
- *repressing things about ourselves that we do not accept;*
- *asserting our identity before others;*
- *seeking revenge on those who have hurt us;*
- *running away from issues we don't want to face.*

As a result we are tired, and when our friends come to us for help in their time of agony, they find us asleep.

'In silence the veil of the passions is removed and the eyes of the heart begin naturally to gaze on the mysteries of the Kingdom.'

John Cassian

Lord, we have many noble desires but not the strength to implement them.
We must watch and pray so that we can go beyond the flesh and experience the power of the Spirit within us.

Second Sorrowful Mystery

The Scourging at the Pillar

GOSPEL TEXT

Matthew 27:11-26
Jesus before Pilate

Jesus, then, was brought before the governor, and the governor put to him this question, 'Are you the king of Jews?' Jesus replied, 'It is you who say it.' But when he was accused by the chief priests and the elders he refused to answer at all. Pilate then said to him, 'Do you not hear how many charges they have made against you?' But to the governor's amazement, he offered not a word in answer to any of the charges.

At festival time it was the governor's practice to release a prisoner for the people, anyone they chose. Now there was then a notorious prisoner whose name was Barabbas. So when the crowd gathered, Pilate said to them, 'Which do you want me to release for you: Barabbas, or Jesus who is called Christ?' For Pilate knew it was out of jealousy that they had handed him over.

Now, as he was seated in the chair of judgment, his wife sent him a message, 'Have nothing to do with the upright man; I have been extremely upset today by a dream I had about him.'

The chief priests and the elders, however, had persuaded the crowd to demand the release of Barabbas and the execution of Jesus. So when the governor spoke and asked them, 'Which of the two do you want me to release for you?' they said, 'Barabbas'. Pilate said to them, 'But in that case, what am I to do with Jesus who is called Christ?' They all said, 'Let him be crucified!' He asked, 'But what harm has he done?' But they shouted all the louder, 'Let him be crucified!' Then Pilate saw that he was making no impression, that in fact a riot was imminent. So he took some water, washed his hands in front of the crowd and said, 'I am innocent of this man's blood. It is your concern'. And the people, every one of them, shouted back, 'Let his blood be on us and on our children!' Then he released Barabbas for them. After having Jesus scourged he handed him over to be crucified.

MEDITATION

The gospel accounts of the passion of Jesus give little attention to his physical sufferings. They concentrate more on the fact that he was rejected and humiliated, as had been foretold by the prophets, especially Isaiah.

A good example is the account of the scourging at the pillar. In the custom of the time, scourging was the prelude to crucifixion. It was probably a way of ensuring that the one to be crucified was weakened and so would not last long on the cross.

The mystery of the scourging is best understood, therefore, as the moment when the decision was finally taken that Jesus would be crucified. It was the climax of the long, humiliating process by which he was rejected by the people.

As in the first mystery, we can focus on Jesus or on those who rejected him. Each of the characters represents a specific role – Pilate, the chief priests and elders, and the people as a whole. The wife of Pilate is a woman and a pagan, on both counts a symbol of the 'little ones' who have a wisdom that is hidden from 'the learned and the clever' (*Matthew 11:25*).

PRAYERS

'The crowds will be astonished at him, and kings stand speechless before him, for they shall see something never told, and witness something never heard before.'

Isaiah 52:15

Lord, when chief priests and elders bring charges against us, we may offer no reply exteriorly but within our hearts we do.

Only those who, like Jesus, trust you totally, refuse to answer at all.

'To be non-aggressive physically but dynamically aggressive spiritually.'

Martin Luther King

Lord, those who follow the way of Jesus continue to arouse hostility on the part of oppressive rulers who bring many charges against them.

Lord, forgive us that like Pilate we abdicate our responsibilities:
- *we leave hard decisions about our children to our spouse;*
- *we ignore injustice in our workplace;*
- *we don't defend our friends when they are criticised.*

Eventually it becomes a habit and when we see innocent people condemned we take some water and wash our hands, saying that we are innocent of the injustice that is being done.

'On him lies a punishment that brings us peace and through his wounds we are healed.'

Isaiah 53:5

Lord, we think today of those who have lost control of their lives:
- *old and unable to look after themselves;*
- *without a job;*
- *in prison.*

Their greatest suffering is to know that others are deciding their fate not with objectivity but in their own interests.

May those suffering be healed by the memory that on Good Friday morning in Pilate's praetorium Jesus felt as they do.

'The poor are the sad cortège trailing behind all conflicts; it is the injustices committed against the poor which occasion and fuel conflicts.'

Pope John Paul II, Assisi, January 1993

Lord, when leaders influence their people to let Barabbas, the
violent one, loose in the world,
as sure as anything the shedding of blood falls upon them and their
children.

Third Sorrowful Mystery
The Crowning with Thorns

GOSPEL TEXT

Matthew 27:27-31

Then the governor's soldiers took Jesus with them into the praetorium and collected the whole cohort round him. And they stripped him and put a scarlet cloak round him, and having twisted some thorns into a crown they put this on his head and placed a reed in his right hand. To make fun of him they knelt to him saying 'Hail King of the Jews!' And they spat on him and took the reed and struck him on the head with it. And when they had finished making fun of him, they took off the cloak and dressed him in his own clothes and led him away to crucifixion.

MEDITATION

As in the previous mystery, so in this one, the gospel account focuses not on the physical suffering but on the humiliation of Jesus.

Irony is a consistent theme in St Matthew's account of the passion: Jesus is arrested but he is supremely free, he is on trial but he is the one who is judging.

Our meditations on this mystery can focus on the irony involved: the soldiers think they are mocking Jesus whereas they are revealing the kind of king he is.

This whole passage is a fulfilment of the prophecies of Isaiah, especially *50:6* and *52:14*.

PRAYERS

'It is not as if we have a high priest who is incapable of feeling our weaknesses with us; but we have one who has been tempted in every way that we are, though he is without sin.'

Hebrews 4:15

Lord, we remember a time when we were humiliated:
- *we failed an examination;*
- *we were betrayed by a friend;*
- *we were caught committing a sin.*

We felt stripped and made to wear a scarlet cloak,
the crown on our head was made of thorns
the sceptre in our right hand a reed,
our subjects mockingly knelt to us and called us king.
Only Jesus understood.

'The saints find no time for the glamour of jewellery and the elegance of dress for their whole attention is fixed on improving and adorning the inward self.'

St Bernard

Lord, do not let us seek earthly crowns.
Before we know it, the crown turns out to be a twisted ring of thorns,
what looked a beautiful sceptre becomes a reed to strike us on the head with,
those who up to a short while ago were our subjects, now kneel to us in mockery.

'What a happy outcome that this tyrant who would hammer the lowly into subjection should unwittingly be fashioning their eternal crowns for them.'

St Bernard

Lord, we think of those unjustly mocked:
- *young people who have high moral standards;*
- *victims of racism;*
- *battered wives and children.*

Let Jesus teach them that the scarlet cloak can really be a royal robe, the reed a real sceptre,

that those who kneel in mockery are really reverencing them and a time must come when they will no longer make fun of them.

Fourth Sorrowful Mystery
Jesus carries his cross

GOSPEL TEXT

Matthew 27:32-38

On their way out, they came across a man from Cyrene, called Simon, and enlisted him to carry his cross. When they had reached a place called Golgotha, that is the place of the skull, they gave him wine to drink mixed with gall, which he tasted but refused to drink. When they had finished crucifying him they shared out his clothing by casting lots, and then sat down and stayed there keeping guard over him. Above his head was placed the charge against him; it read: 'This is Jesus, the King of the Jews'. Then two bandits were crucified with him, one on the right and one on the left.

MEDITATION

This mystery contains all the events that led up to the crucifixion of Jesus.

Whereas St John *(19:17)* says that Jesus carried the cross himself, all three synoptics say that Simon of Cyrene was enlisted to carry it. Christian piety came up with the compromise that Simon merely 'helped' Jesus carry the cross but this is not in any text. For the synoptics, Simon is the symbol of Jesus' teaching that those who want to follow him must take up his cross.

The title 'place of the skull' is ironical, since it was this place which brought new life to the world.

The drink offered to Jesus is a fulfilment of *Psalm 31:6,* and the sharing out of his clothes of *Psalm 22:18.* Reading these verses will help our meditation.

There is irony in the guards keeping watch over Jesus when no human power could restrain him, and in the placard proclaiming the truth though it was meant to be a mockery.

Jesus among robbers fulfils *Isaiah 53:9* and *12.*

Prayers
Lord, we think today of those who bear the sufferings of others:
- *parents of children with handicaps looking frantically for a school for them;*
- *leaders trying in vain to get employment or housing for those in need;*
- *relief workers in Somalia and Sudan.*

They are Simons of Cyrene whom you have enlisted to carry the cross of Jesus.

'**The gravest sin committed against our country is to have classified the struggle of the Guatemalan people as the work of communists.**'

Rigoberta Menchu, Nobel Peace Prize winner

Lord, how often in recent years we have seen the strange spectacle of evil-doers sitting down and staying to keep guard over the innocent:
- *Gandhi, Nelson Mandela and Lech Walesa in prison;*
- *leaders of basic Christian communities denounced as terrorists;*
- *the Church persecuted as subversive.*

Ironically it was the jailers who were threats to the world,
and those who shared out the clothing of their victims were naked.

Lord, forgive us for passing hasty judgments on others:
- *those who minister to prostitutes;*
- *those who choose the single life;*
- *priests and religious who get involved in politics or trade unions.*

Thus did people pass judgment on Jesus when they saw him crucified with two robbers one on his right and one on his left.

40

Lord we think of people who are victims of AIDS.
Like Jesus, their deepest suffering is to be rejected by families and
friends,
crucified with evil-doers on the right and on the left.

Lord, our Church today is too concerned with being respectable.
Teach us that you have enlisted us to carry the cross of Jesus,
to go with him as far as the place of the skull,
to have our clothing shared out and to be numbered among
evil-doers.

Fifth Sorrowful Mystery

The crucifixion

GOSPEL TEXT

Matthew 27:39-50

The passers-by jeered at him; they shook their heads and said, 'So you would destroy the Temple and in three days rebuild it! Then save yourself if you are God's son and come down from the cross!' The chief priests with the scribes and elders mocked him in the same way, with the words, 'He saved others; he cannot save himself. He is the king of Israel; let him come down from the cross now, and we will believe in him. He has put his trust in God; now let God rescue him if he wants him. For he did say, "I am God's son".' Even the bandits who were crucified with him taunted him in the same way.

From the sixth hour there was darkness over all the land until the ninth hour. And about the ninth hour, Jesus cried out in a loud voice, 'Eli, eli, lama sabachthani?' that is, 'My God, my God, why have you forsaken me?' When some of those who stood there heard this, they said, 'The man is calling on Elijah', and one of them quickly ran to get a sponge which he filled with vinegar and putting it on a reed, gave it to him to drink. But the rest of them said, 'Wait! And see if Elijah will come to save him'. But Jesus, again crying out in a loud voice, yielded up his spirit.

MEDITATION

Our meditation on the mocking of Jesus in *verses 39-44* will be enriched if we keep in mind the mocking in the third mystery; each passage can help us interpret the other.

There is a parallel, too, between these verses and the temptation of Jesus in *Matthew 4:1-11*.

It is interesting that Matthew's account knows nothing of the 'good thief' mentioned in *Luke 23:39-43*.

The cry of Jesus in *verse 46* is the first verse of the great *Psalm 22,* which expresses the terrible anguish of God's chosen one but also his unconquerable trust in God.

Matthew's words describing the death of Jesus, 'he yielded up his spirit', are very significant.

Prayers
'From Somalia to Sarajevo,
Children with eyes that stare,
A thousand miles, cry tears of excrement and blood.'
> David Rudder, 'Calypso', *The Ministry of Rhythm*

Lord, when we look around the world today and see children being crucified:
* *victims of war;*
* *inheritors of AIDS;*
* *on the streets of Brazil;*
* *abandoned by their parents;*
we cry out to you, wondering why you have deserted your people,
and we thank you that Jesus is crying out with us.

Lord, human beings can become so hard-hearted.
they can see innocent people suffering and when others run to get a sponge dipped in vinegar and give them to drink,
harden their hearts and say no, wait and see if an angel will come to save them.

'This is the seeing that consists in not seeing, because that which we seek transcends all knowledge.'
> St Gregory of Nyssa

Lord, you invite us from time to time to make the journey to our
deep selves beyond all that gives us security:
- *the love of family and friends;*
- *our accomplishments at work;*
- *our virtues;*

so that we can experience only our poverty and our trust in your
love.
Then like Jesus on the cross we can cry out in a loud voice and yield
up our spirit to you.

Lord, depression is a terrible experience,
we who have saved many others cannot save ourselves,
we have a placard over our heads proclaiming that we are royal
people, but it is only a mockery,
we hear voices within us taunting us, we put our trust in God, now
let him rescue us.
Even those who suffer with us seem to taunt us in the same way.
There seems to be darkness over the whole earth, and we can only
cry out in a loud voice,
My God, my God, why have you forsaken me?

'God's foolishness is wiser than human wisdom, and God's
weakness is stronger than human strength.'

1 Corinthians 1:25

Lord, the judgments of the world are as false today as they were on
Calvary.
It is because we are your children that we don't need to come down
from the cross,
those who are not concerned to save themselves are the only ones
who can save others,
when we truly put our trust in you, you do not have to rescue us,
the crucified King of Israel is totally trustworthy.

The Glorious Mysteries

I am proposing the *Epistle to the Ephesians* as the scriptural background to these meditations. Extracts have been chosen for each mystery but it would be beneficial to read the whole epistle as a starting-point for the meditation.

Ephesians is one of the late writings of the New Testament and is therefore the fruit of several generations of Christians reflecting on the story of Jesus.

During these years, Christians were able to see ever more clearly that the death and resurrection of Jesus broke down barriers within humanity. At that time the important barrier was the one which separated Jews from Greeks. Today Jesus is breaking down other barriers.

By the time of *Ephesians,* the Christians also saw more clearly that the story of Jesus had implications for the whole of creation, an insight that remains important for us today.

First Glorious Mystery

The Resurrection

Ephesians 1:17-2:10

May the God of our Lord Jesus Christ, the Father of Glory, give you a spirit of wisdom and perception of what is revealed, to bring you to full knowledge of him. May he enlighten the eyes of your mind so that you can see what hope his call holds for you, how rich is the glory of the heritage he offers among his only people, and how extraordinarily great is the power that he has exercised for us believers; this accords with the strength of his power at work in him at his right hand, in heaven, far above every principality, ruling force, power or sovereignty, or any other name that can be named, not only in this age but also in the age to come. *He has put all things under his feet,* and made him, as he is above all things, the head of the Church, which is his Body, the fullness of him who is filled, all in all.

And you were dead, through the crimes and the sins which used to make up your way of life when you were living by the principles of this world, obeying the ruler who dominates the air, the spirit who is at work in those who rebel. We too were all among them once, living only by our natural inclinations obeying the demands of human self-indulgence and our own whim; our nature made us no less liable to God's retribution than the rest of the world. But God, being rich in faithful love, through the great love with which he loves us, even when we were dead in our sins, brought us to life with Christ – it is through grace that you have been saved – and raised us up with him and gave us a place with him in heaven, in Christ Jesus.

This was to show for all ages to come, through his goodness towards us in Christ Jesus, how extraordinarily rich he is in grace. Because it is by grace that you have been saved, through faith; not by anything of yours, but by a gift from God; not by anything you have done, so that nobody can claim the credit. We are God's work of art, created in Christ Jesus for the good works which God has already designated to make up our way of life.

MEDITATION

This passage invites us to enter into the 'mystery' of the resurrection of Jesus.

The Christians understood from the beginning that the resurrection was something that happened not only to Jesus but to his followers as well.

As early as the epistle to the Romans, St Paul could say, *'when we were baptised we went into the tomb with him and joined him in death, so that as Christ was raised from the dead by the Father's glory we too might live a new life'* (6:4).

In these verses too, St Paul celebrates that we have been raised to a life of grace and of union with the risen Lord. He adds that it is also the life of the people of God in the Church.

In keeping with the added insights of the Church, Paul stresses that grace brings insight and wisdom.

He also stresses that the resurrection (both Jesus' and ours) is a free and generous gift of God.

PRAYERS

'He is not here for he has risen as he said he would.'

Matthew 28:6

Lord, we thank you for the strength of your power,
that power by which you raised Jesus from the dead to
make him sit at your right hand in heaven,
far above every sovereignty, authority, power and domination,
above any other name that can be named not only in this age but
in the age to come.

'Not all are called to be hermits, but we all need enough silence and solitude in our lives to allow the deep inner voice of our true selves to be heard.'

Thomas Merton

Lord, there was a time when we were dead through the crimes and sins in which we used to live:
- *we were following the ways of this world,*
  obeying the ruler who governs the air, the spirit who is at work in the rebellious;
- *we lived a sensual life, ruled entirely by our physical desires and our own ideas,*
  as much under your anger as the rest of the world.
We thank you that you were generous with your mercy,
- *called us to experience our life in Christ;*
- *raised us up with him and gave us a place with you in heaven in Christ Jesus.*

'The society needs more than research, we need a quantum leap into a new confidence, a new culture.'

Winston Dookeran, West Indian economist

Lord, forgive us that we give up hope, believing:
- *that this person will always be an addict;*
- *that we will not be able to forgive;*
- *that our country will not get out of its mess.*
Give us a spirit of wisdom so that we can understand the mystery of the resurrection of Jesus, and can come to full knowledge of you.
Enlighten the eyes of our minds, so that we can see what hope your call holds for us,
what rich glories you have promised we will inherit
and how infinitely great is the power that you have
exercised for us believers.

'When one sees eternity in things that pass away and infinity in finite things, then one has gained pure knowledge.'

Bhagavad Gita

Lord, give us the spirit of wisdom and perception,
enlighten the eyes of our minds,
so that we can see in all things the fullness of him who fills all creation.

'When people are weak and defenceless, I must raise my voice on their behalf.'

Pope John Paul II

Lord, preserve your Church from seeking power for its own sake.
Grant that we may seek only the infinitely great power which you exercise,
the power which you use to raise up the lowly and make them sit at your right hand.

Second Glorious Mystery

The Ascension

GOSPEL TEXT

Ephesians 4:7-16

On each one of us God's favour has been bestowed in whatever way Christ allotted it. That is why it says:

> He went up to the heights, took captives,
> he gave gifts to humanity.

When it says, 'he went up', it must mean that he had gone down to the deepest levels of the earth. The one who went down is none other than the one who went up above all the heavens to fill all things. And to some, his 'gift' was that they should be apostles; to some prophets; to some, evangelists; to some, pastors and teachers; to knit God's holy people together for the work of service to build up the Body of Christ, until we all reach unity in faith and knowledge of the Son of God and form the perfect Man fully mature with the fullness of Christ himself. Then we shall no longer be children, or tossed one way and another, and carried hither and thither by every new gust of teaching, at the mercy of all the tricks people play and their unscrupulousness in deliberate deception. If we live by the truth and in love we shall grow completely into the Christ, who is the head by whom the whole body is fitted and joined together, every joint adding its own strength, for each individual part to work according to its function. So the body grows until it has built itself up in love.

MEDITATION

In this passage St Paul invites us to use *Psalm 68* as the starting point for our meditation on the mystery of the Ascension. He refers to *verse 18* but it would be good to read the whole psalm in order to get a feel for it.

In *Psalm 68* the psalmist celebrates a victory of God's grace and this is St Paul's interpretation of the Ascension, seeing it as the sign that Jesus had won the victory over all the forces of evil. In our meditation, we celebrate Jesus' victory over a particular manifestation of evil that we are sensitive to at this moment.

St Paul stresses that Jesus won the victory because he had *'descended to the lower regions of the earth'*, a point well expressed in the famous hymn of praise in *Philippians 2:6-11*.

St Paul shows also that Jesus' victory was not for himself but consisted in his *'giving gifts to men'*.

PRAYERS

'He descended into hell, he ascended into heaven.'

Apostles' Creed

Lord, we thank you that your son Jesus descended right down to the lower regions of the earth and that he has now risen higher than all the heavens to fill all things.

'The modern world seems in some ways to create a delusion that we do not, perhaps even that we ought not, to suffer.'

Vicky Cosstick, English spiritual writer

Lord, we think today of those who are resentful that they are experiencing rejection from friends and colleagues.
Help them to see that it is not possible to give gifts to others while remaining comfortable and that those who ascend to give gifts must be none other than those who descend to the lower regions of the earth.
When we plumb the depths of lowliness through:
* *failure in enterprises that we had set our hearts on;*
* *destructive criticism from those we look to for support;*
* *faults in ourselves that we have condemned in others;*
when we discover the old enemies still there within us – lust, self-

righteousness, the desire to control,
only then can we make them captive and only then give gifts to
others.

Lord, we thank you for sending us great people like Jesus.
While they were with us they were the centre of our reverence and
admiration.
Then the time came when they moved on and we saw that each of
us had also been given our own share of grace.

'Lord God, you are like a weaver in our lives.
You have spun each one of us
Into a unique and colourful strand,
With our own special hue and texture.
Then you wove us together
Into your human family,
Blanketing the globe.'

Meditation for Women's World Day of Prayer

Lord, now that Jesus has ascended into heaven
we have all been given our own share of grace,
given as he has allotted it to us,
so that together we make a unity in the work of service,
building up his Body.

'We are all pilgrims, members of the people of God whom the
Creator and Father leads towards his own holiness.'

Pope John Paul II in India, 1986

Lord, your son Jesus has completed his journey by ascending into
heaven where he is seated at your right hand.
Remind us that we are not yet there,
we are only on our way, building up your body until we become
fully mature with the fullness of Christ himself.

Third Glorious Mystery

The Descent of the Holy Spirit on the Apostles

GOSPEL TEXT

Ephesians 5:8-20

You were darkness once, but now you are light in the Lord; behave as children of light, for the effects of the light are seen in complete goodness and uprightness and truth. Try to discover what the Lord wants of you, take no part in the futile works of darkness but, on the contrary, show them up for what they are. The things which are done in secret are shameful even to speak of; but anything shown up by the light will be illuminated and anything illuminated is itself a light. That is why it is said:

> Wake up, sleeper,
> rise from the dead,
> and Christ will shine on you.

So be very careful about the sort of lives you lead, like intelligent and not like senseless people. Make the best of the present time, for it is a wicked age. This is why you must not be thoughtless but must recognise what is the will of the Lord. *Do not get drunk with wine;* this is simple dissipation; be filled with the Spirit. Sing psalms and hymns and inspired songs among yourselves, singing and chanting to the Lord in your hearts, always and everywhere giving thanks to God who is our Father in the name of our Lord Jesus Christ.

MEDITATION

This passage from Ephesians is a meditation on the fruits of the coming of the Spirit upon the followers of Jesus. Here again the meditation is the result of many years of experience of Christian living.

The passage is in two sections:

verses 8-14   teaching on the enlightenment brought by the Spirit;

verses 15-20   moral exhortation to life in the Spirit.

The theme of light is very important in the New Testament, the gospels as well as the epistles. In the first years of Christianity, enlightenment was a name for baptism.

The passage teaches that enlightenment brings wisdom, *'knowing what the Lord wants'* and leads to life, *'rising from the dead'*. It is not merely theoretical, however, but involves *'having nothing to do with the works of darkness'*. It also requires getting involved in the world and *'redeeming it'*.

The moral section speaks of an interior life of recollection, the opposite of 'dissipation'.

PRAYERS

'Tongues of fire separated and came to rest on the head of each of them.'

Acts 2:3

Lord, we thank you for sending your Holy Spirit on the apostles at the feast of Pentecost.
They had been darkness but now they were light in you,
children of light, with the effects of the light seen in right living and truth.
Their lives were now illuminated and they had nothing more to do with the futile works of darkness.
They were now awake from their sleep and risen from the dead.
Christ was now shining on them.

'When the deed of virtue seems to happen by itself, simply because we love goodness and for no other reason, then we are virtuous and not before.'

Meister Eckhart

Lord, we remember the time when quite suddenly we became
aware of how much we were guided by lust, resentment, or the
desire to control others.
All the time we had been doing it in secret, ashamed to admit it.
Now the truth of ourselves had been illuminated by the Holy Spirit
and had been turned into light.
Thank you, Lord.

'The Group of Seven should be setting an example, but all it
can offer is platitudes.'

Jacques Delors,
former president of the European Commission

Lord, send your Holy Spirit on the leaders of our time:
- *on the world stage;*
- *in our country and local community;*
- *in the Church, schools, families.*

So often they accept an evil situation as inevitable or even as good.
Help them to see what you want of them,
so that having nothing to do with futile works of darkness they may
expose them,
and the shameful things which are being done in secret,
may be exposed to the light.

Lord, we pray for those who are bowed down by discouragement or
depression.
Wake them from their sleep, raise them from the dead, so that
Christ may shine on them.

'This is Port of Spain to me, a city ideal in its commercial and
human proportions, where a citizen is a walker, not a
pedestrian.'

Derek Walcott,
accepting the Nobel Prize for Literature, December 1992

*Lord, we pray that we may construct a world where all feel
themselves respected for who they are,
awake from their sleep, risen from the dead and the light of Christ
shining on them.*

'God sent his son into the world, not to condemn the world,
but so that through him the world might be saved.'

John 3:17

*Lord, forgive us that we dwell on the evils of the modern world,
continually denouncing them from our pulpits and in our
conversation.
The descent of the Spirit on the apostles taught us that your grace is
at work in the world
and even if this is a wicked age, our lives should redeem it.*

'The Church has in its possession, under lock and key, the
purest gold of mystical religion.'

Alan Watts, English spiritual writer

*Lord, we thank you for the beautiful experiences of liturgical
prayer, when we are together and sing the words and tunes of
psalms and hymns.
Lead us to go beyond this external liturgy and enter the presence of
the Holy Spirit within us, so that we can go on singing and
chanting to you in our hearts,
and always and everywhere be giving thanks to you who are our
Father, in the name of our Lord Jesus Christ.*

'Sometimes people ask me, how do you cope? I say, I don't,
but I don't worry about it.'

Archbishop Pantin
in an interview to mark his silver jubilee as a bishop

Lord, one of the fruits of the Spirit is that always and everywhere we are giving thanks to you, our Father, in the name of the Lord Jesus Christ.

Fourth Glorious Mystery

The Assumption of the Blessed Virgin Mary into Heaven

GOSPEL TEXT

Ephesians 5:25-27

Husbands should love their wives, just as Christ loved the Church and sacrificed himself for her to make her holy by washing her in cleansing water with a form of words, so that when he took the Church to himself she would be glorious, with no speck or wrinkle or anything like that, but holy and faultless.

MEDITATION

As with all the mysteries of the Rosary, in celebrating Mary's assumption into heaven, we celebrate our own destiny.

As the Vatican Council expressed it, *'she is hailed as a pre-eminent and altogether singular member of the Church and as the Church's model and excellent exemplar in faith and charity.'*

In Mary's assumption then *'the Church has already reached that perfection where she exists without spot or wrinkle'*. We see her as our hope since *'the followers of Christ still strive to increase in holiness by conquering sin'*.

The passage teaches that Mary's grace came as a result of Jesus' sacrifice. The metaphor of cleansing is appropriate. In our case (not in Mary's since she was conceived immaculate) it also reminds us of our baptism.

St Paul sees marriage as a powerful symbol of Christ's sacrificial, cleansing love.

PRAYERS

Lord, we thank you that your son Jesus loved his mother Mary.

He sacrificed himself for her, to make her holy,
he made her clean, so that when he took her to himself she was
glorious, with no speck or wrinkle or anything like that, but holy
and faultless.

'It is through reconciliation that we regain our humanity. To
work for reconciliation is to live to show others what their
humanity is.'

> Joe Seramane, Christian leader from South Africa
> meeting those who had tortured him in prison

Lord, when we sacrifice ourselves by letting go of anger,
resentment and the desire for revenge,
we share in Jesus' work of cleansing humanity,
and preparing it for you to take it to yourself.

'Words can do anything,
words can make you feel like a king.'

> 'Words', by calypsonian Baron

Lord, as we contemplate Mary assumed into heaven, we remember
the addicts in our society.
Help us to remember that Jesus sacrifices himself for them too,
to make them holy,
and you want us to minister to them by washing and in the form of
words,
so that when the time comes for you to take them to yourself, they
too might be without speck or wrinkle but holy and faultless.

Lord, we pray for couples who are having difficulties in their
marriage,
especially those who feel that their relationship is going nowhere.
We pray that through the intercession of Mary, their pain may
become a sacrifice, by which they will make each other clean.

'A woman in childbirth suffers because her time has come, but when she has given birth to the child she forgets her suffering, in her joy that a man has been born into the world.'

John 16:21

Lord, we thank you for the miracle of childbirth.
The mother's pains are like a baptism, cleansing waters out of which she takes her baby to herself, glorious and holy.

Fifth Glorious Mystery

The Crowning of Mary as Queen of Heaven

GOSPEL TEXT

Ephesians 1:3-12

Blessed be God, the Father of our Lord Jesus Christ,
who has blessed us with all the spiritual blessings of heaven in
Christ.
Thus he chose us in Christ before the world was made
to be holy and faultless before him in love,
marking us out for himself beforehand, to be adopted sons,
through Jesus Christ.
Such was his purpose and good pleasure,
to the praise of the glory of his grace,
his free gift to us in the beloved,
in whom, through his blood, we gain our freedom,
the forgiveness of our sins.
Such is the richness of the grace which he has showered on us
in all wisdom and insight.
He has let us know the mystery of his purpose,
according to his good pleasure which he determined beforehand
in Christ,
for him to act upon when the times had run their course:
that he would bring everything together under Christ, as head,
everything in the heavens and everything on earth.
And it is in him that we have received our heritage,
marked out beforehand as we were,
under the plan of the One who guides all things
as he decided by his own will,
chosen to be,
for the praise of his glory,
the people who would put their hopes in Christ before he came.

MEDITATION

The Vatican Council said of this mystery, *'Mary was exalted by the Lord as Queen of all, in order that she might be the more thoroughly conformed to her Son, the Lord of lords and the conqueror of sin and death'.*

It is also said that she is *'the image and first flowering of the Church as she is to be perfected in the world to come'.*

The crowning of Mary is therefore well-expressed in this opening passage of Ephesians in which St Paul celebrates the glorious destiny of humanity in Jesus Christ.

PRAYERS

Lord, we thank you that you have blessed Mary with all the spiritual blessings of heaven in Christ.
Before the world was made, you chose her in Christ, to be holy and spotless and to live through love in your presence.
Such is the richness of the grace which you have showered on her in all wisdom and insight,
so that in Christ you have brought all things under her,
things in heaven and things on earth.
In him you claimed her as your own,
chosen from the beginning, under your pre-determined plan chosen to be for your greater glory, a model of those who put their hope in Christ before he came.

'When I walk with Jesus, he always leads me to the poorest, the lowliest, and the lost, so that I may open my heart to them.'

Jean Vanier

Lord, we pray that your Church may have as its special ministry to help the outcasts of society look up to Mary crowned as queen of heaven,

and to become aware that they too have been blessed with all the
spiritual blessings in Christ,
that you chose them too to be holy and spotless and to live through
love in your presence
and that in Christ all things have been brought under them, things
in heaven and things on earth.

'We have to walk on through the darkness. I don't know
where we are going but I think the Lord knows.'

Cardinal Hume of Westminister
as he celebrated his seventieth birthday

Lord, we pray that when we feel we are drifting aimlessly,
as individuals, as a Church, or a culture,
we may contemplate Mary in her glory,
and so remember your hidden plan so kindly made in Christ from
the beginning,
to act upon when the times have run their course to the end,
to bring everything under Christ as head, everything in heaven and
everything on earth.

Lord, we thank you for artists who through your gifts can raise us
up to experience that we are your chosen ones,
chosen to be holy and spotless and to live through love in your
presence,
that we have gained our freedom and the forgiveness of our sins.

'I am not going to let the chemotherapy manage me, I'm
going to manage it.'

Cancer patient

Lord, we thank you for the courage which comes from knowing that
through the Blood of Christ we have gained our freedom and
forgiveness of our sins,

and that when the times have run their course to the end,
you will bring everything together under Christ as head,
everything in the heavens and everything on earth.

Lord, forgive us that we presume to judge who are those you have
chosen to be blessed with all the spiritual blessings of heaven in
Christ.
Mary in her glory reminds us of all those chosen for your greater
glory, the people who have put their hopes in Christ before he comes
to them.